ESSENTIAL CONCEPTS IN COMPUTER SCIENCE

COLLABORATION IN COMPUTER SCIENCE

WORKING TOGETHER

JONATHAN BARD

PowerKiDS press.
New York

Published in 2019 by The Rosen Publishing Group, Inc.
29 East 21st Street, New York, NY 10010

First Edition

Editor: Jane Katirgis
Book Design: Reann Nye

Photo Credits: Cover cobalt88/Shutterstock.com; p. 5 asiseeit/E+/Getty Images; p. 7 https://commons.wikimedia.org/wiki/File:Mission_control_center.jpg; p. 9 Monkey Business Images/Shutterstock.com; p. 11 Mat Hayward/Shutterstock.com; p. 12 PAKULA PIOTR/Shutterstock.com; p. 13 Hero Images/Getty Images; p. 14 Everett Historical/Shutterstock.com; p. 15 nd3000/Shutterstock.com; p. 16 https://commons.wikimedia.org/wiki/File:H96566k.jpg; p. 17 GaudiLab/Shutterstock.com; p. 19 Africa Studio/Shutterstock.com; p. 21 Luke Schmidt/Shutterstock.com; p. 23 Pressmaster/Shutterstock.com; p. 25 g-stockstudio/Shutterstock.com; p. 26 garagestock/Shutterstock.com; p. 27 Uber Images/Shutterstock.com; pp. 29, 30 Rawpixel.com/Shutterstock.com.

Cataloging-in-Publication Data

Names: Bard, Jonathan.
Title: Collaboration in computer science / Jonathan Bard.
Description: New York : PowerKids Press, 2019. | Series: Essential concepts in computer science | Includes index.
Identifiers: LCCN ISBN 9781538331675 (pbk.) | ISBN 9781538331651 (library bound) | ISBN 9781538331682 (6 pack)
Subjects: LCSH: Computer programming–Juvenile literature. | Application software–Juvenile literature.
Classification: LCC QA76.52 B37 2019 | DDC 005.1–dc23

Manufactured in the United States of America

CPSIA Compliance Information: Batch #CS18PK: For Further Information contact Rosen Publishing, New York, New York at 1-800-237-9932

CONTENTS

TEAMWORK!

Computers and smartphones make our lives easier, and they are fun to use. But did you know that it takes huge teams of people to write the **code** to make them work? Computer scientists, programmers, and testers **collaborate** as a team to work on projects.

You've probably worked on a team, too. At school, you may read a book with a group or solve math problems as a class. Those are great examples of collaboration. You and your classmates are working and learning together.

Working together is useful in many different jobs. It is really important in computer science because writing code is hard. It takes many people with different skills for a project to be successful.

Working in a group at school is a great example of collaboration. >

ZONE
NO FOOD OR
DRINK

BUILDING SOFTWARE REQUIRES A TEAM

Computers need code to work. Writing code takes a team of people with different skills. At the start of a project, companies organize people into teams to work together to complete it.

Project managers are people who know how to set up and manage a team of computer programmers. The managers keep the project on schedule. They also help other members of the team—such as coders, testers, and designers—work together. A project manager is one of the team leaders and is responsible for the success of the project.

Also key to the team is the **software engineer**. This person has a lot of experience writing code and is able to help the team solve hard problems.

COMPUTER CONNECTION

The Bureau of Labor Statistics says that, as of 2016, there were an estimated 1.6 million software developers and programmers in the United States. That's a lot of people writing code!

The National Aeronautics and Space Administration (NASA) has a large team of computer programmers and scientists working on space missions.

STARTING A NEW PROJECT

The first step to a successful computer science project is having a project to work on. A **client**, or the person with an idea for a project, meets with the team and talks about the idea. By talking it over, the team can figure out what needs to be done, what it will cost, and whether it is possible.

The team talks with the client many times when a project is getting started. Sometimes a client makes changes or comes up with new ideas. By talking often, everyone can make sure they have a good plan. The more the team talks about their progress and ideas, the more likely it is the project will be successful. Eventually, the team decides if the project should continue to the next steps.

Senior members of the team meet a client—often face-to-face—to discuss new projects and share ideas.

WHAT NEEDS TO BE DONE?

Once everyone has talked about the idea, the team is ready to make a detailed plan. This step is called requirement gathering, and it's at this point that everything the program needs to do is written down. That way, when the team starts writing code, they have **guidelines** to follow. This is similar to when you receive a test or a homework assignment—reading the directions is the first and most important step.

Gathering requirements for the project can take many meetings, and it can take months or even years! The full list of requirements is sometimes called the **project scope**, which is a detailed list of what needs to be done. The project scope helps keep things organized and gives programmers a clear idea of all the items that need be completed.

Just like programmers have guidelines to follow, students get requirements for their homework. These guidelines explain how to answer the questions. >

TEAM ASSIGNMENTS

Project leaders use the project scope to plan out the work. They try to figure out how long each step will take and how much money it will cost. They also break down big **tasks** into smaller assignments for programmers to work on. This is like when a teacher assigns group projects to the class: each group member takes on one part of the

CREATING GOALS

Setting goals is not just for computer science. You could set a goal to clean your room, learn a language, run a mile, or anything you want to do. Writing down steps that you can do to reach your goal will help you stay organized. It's also rewarding to see progress when you can cross off smaller steps on your list along the way.

Climbing to the top of a mountain is a great example of a goal that takes planning and skills.

assignment, and everyone works together to complete the project on time.

Delegating work is very important, because big projects are too much work for one person to do on their own. Certain tasks, such as coding assignments, often take more time than others. They may also require special skills. The project manager works to assign these more demanding tasks to the right people on the team.

TIME TO CODE: PAIR PROGRAMMING

After the work is divided up and assigned, sometimes two programmers team up to help each other complete one task. This is called **pair programming**, and it's a great way to help prevent mistakes. Usually two people with different skills sit side by side at the same computer, taking turns writing code. The person writing the code is called the driver.

Pair programming works because each programmer has different strengths. Maybe one is really good with math,

COMPUTER CONNECTION

Before modern computers, programs were recorded on pieces of paper called punch cards. These cards were then put into the computer for processing, and results would be printed out for review.

Programmers may work on the same computer to try to solve a tough problem.

while the other is better at design. The designer can help make everything look great, while the math whiz can make sure the math code works correctly.

Working in pairs can be difficult if the two programmers don't communicate. But if they collaborate, the code comes out better!

DEBUGGING AND THE TESTING TEAM

Did you know there are programmers who write code that tests other code? These programmers are called testers. They find any **bugs** that might be hiding in the main code. A *bug* is a fun word coders use to say there's an error in the code.

Testers work closely with the project manager and software engineers to make sure all requirements of the

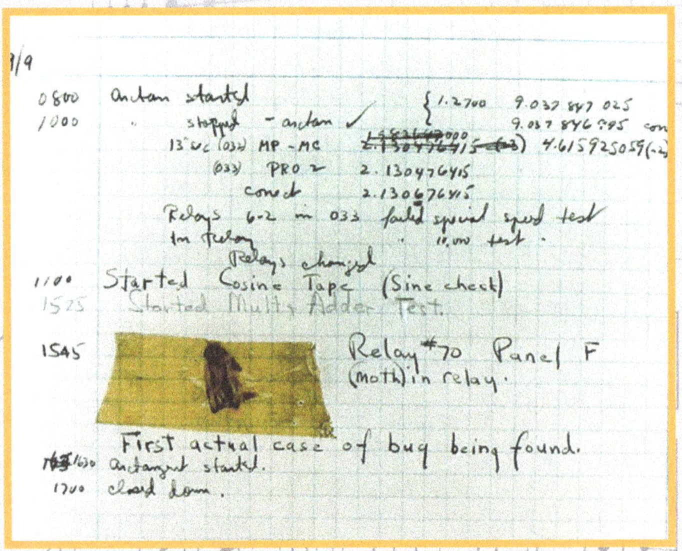

THE FIRST COMPUTER BUG

In 1947, a computer scientist named Grace Murray Hopper was working for the U.S. Navy when she encountered a computer bug. This bug turned out to be an actual moth stuck in the computer! Since then, the term *bug* has been used to talk about errors in code, and the term *debugging* means to find errors. This is Grace Murray Hopper's notebook; she even attached the moth!

Testers are programmers who look for computer bugs that might be hiding in the main code.

program are tested. They think about the end product and write code that the team can use to make sure they are on the right track. It is very important to make sure every piece of code is tested, because this helps prevent errors from making it into the final product. After all, no one likes error messages that stop the program from working!

KEEPING THINGS ORGANIZED: VERSION CONTROL

Keeping everyone up to date is a big challenge. Think of all the people working on the same project. Programmers are writing the main code while testers are writing code for testing. At the same time, other people might be writing directions for the users. It can get very confusing very quickly.

To help keep everyone organized, a tool called **version control** is used. This tool makes sure everyone is using the most up-to-date version of the project. It helps people share changes and progress. It also saves older versions in case someone makes a mistake and they need to go back to an older version. Each programmer is responsible for putting their code into version control, where it can be shared and used by other members of the team.

COMPUTER CONNECTION

Version control is used in other jobs, too. Authors and editors need to keep track of the most current versions of books. Scientists can keep track of their experimental data this way, too.

Version control tools are a lot like bookmarks, marking important pages or, in a programmer's case, important changes.

KEEPING THINGS ON TRACK

Version control systems keep the code organized and the project running smoothly, but making sure everyone is talking to each other is also important. Projects can take several months or years to complete, and new people can be added to the team along the way.

To help all team members stay on track, programmers are encouraged to collaborate and talk to each other often, sometimes every day. Usually these talks happen in short meetings, sometimes called **scrums**, where programmers share their progress and check in on each task. They will also bring up any issues they're facing and share new ideas on how to solve problems. These meetings prevent the team from getting stuck on one issue for too long.

COMPUTER CONNECTION

The popular computer operating system Windows was first released in 1985, which makes it more than thirty years old. It is still being updated today.

The word *scrum* comes from the sport of rugby; it means a bunch of players gathered in a tight formation.

CHECKING IN WITH THE CLIENT

Partway through the process of coding, it is very important to check in with the client and get **feedback**. Sometimes requirements change and new features are needed. It is up to the project manager to take in these changes and figure out what is possible without changing or redoing too much. But remember, the whole point of the project is to take care of what the client needs.

The hardest part of some projects is limiting how much change occurs between the first idea and the final product. It is very important to meet the client's needs, but it is also important to keep the project from growing bigger than planned. The project manager and other leaders must keep the project under control and organized.

THE DREADED SCOPE CREEP!

Clients sometimes like to add or change requirements in the middle of a project. If too many changes are added, programmers use the term *scope creep* to explain why the timeline and budget had to be increased. Adding some features can be a good idea, but avoiding scope creep will keep a project on track to finish on time.

Keeping the project scope under control keeps cost down, timelines on track, and overall quality of the product high.

WORKING TOGETHER TO CROSS THE FINISH LINE

Toward the end of the project, programmers will come together to finish any remaining tasks. They will also make sure they're using the best possible code and edit the program when they need to. Programmers who previously worked together for pair programming may partner with different members of the team to help them with difficult problems. This is called collective code ownership, which means that all members of the team are responsible for the final product. Any programmer can edit code if needed, because each one had a hand in making it. This is just like on a sports team or in a club—it takes a team effort and more than just one person to be successful.

CODE COVERAGE

Because testing code is a very important step, you have to know how good your test code is. One way to measure this is to estimate how much of the main code is being tested. This is called **code coverage**. The goal of the test team is to write tests for as close to 100 percent of the code as possible.

Much like in a race, projects cross the finish line when coding is complete.

ALMOST DONE

The final phase of development is called beta testing. Beta testing is when a small group of users is given access to the final product before anyone else. They use the program as part of their daily lives, as they would if it were a finished product. This is the first real test to see if the code is working as expected. During this test, the programmers get valuable feedback from the

COMPUTER CONNECTION

Beta testing is often used for developing computer games. It's a fun way for people to play a game before it's released to the public, and as they play, information is sent to the programmers.

While clients preview the software, they might find bugs that were originally missed.

client and the testers. This allows the programmers to fix any errors not found by the testing team.

Feedback from the client and testers during the beta test is very important, because this is one of the last chances to make major improvements before the final product is released.

THE FINAL PRODUCT

After all the hard work of planning, writing, and testing code, the project is ready for the real world. However, that does not mean the project is finished. Usually, a small team of programmers will remain on the project to offer user support, fix any new bugs, and provide updates over time. Sometimes a project is supported for many years and many updates.

Maintaining a project is actually very important, because if users have trouble, they need an expert to give them the help they need. You would not want all the hard work that went into the product to go to waste if people have trouble after it is released. Good user support makes your clients happy and your project more successful.

CONTENT PATCHES

Even after a project is released to the client or the public, programmers continue to fix any remaining bugs. Once a bug is fixed, the team has to **patch** the product, which means they send the fixes to the client. If your family has ever updated phones, games, or televisions, you have used a content patch.

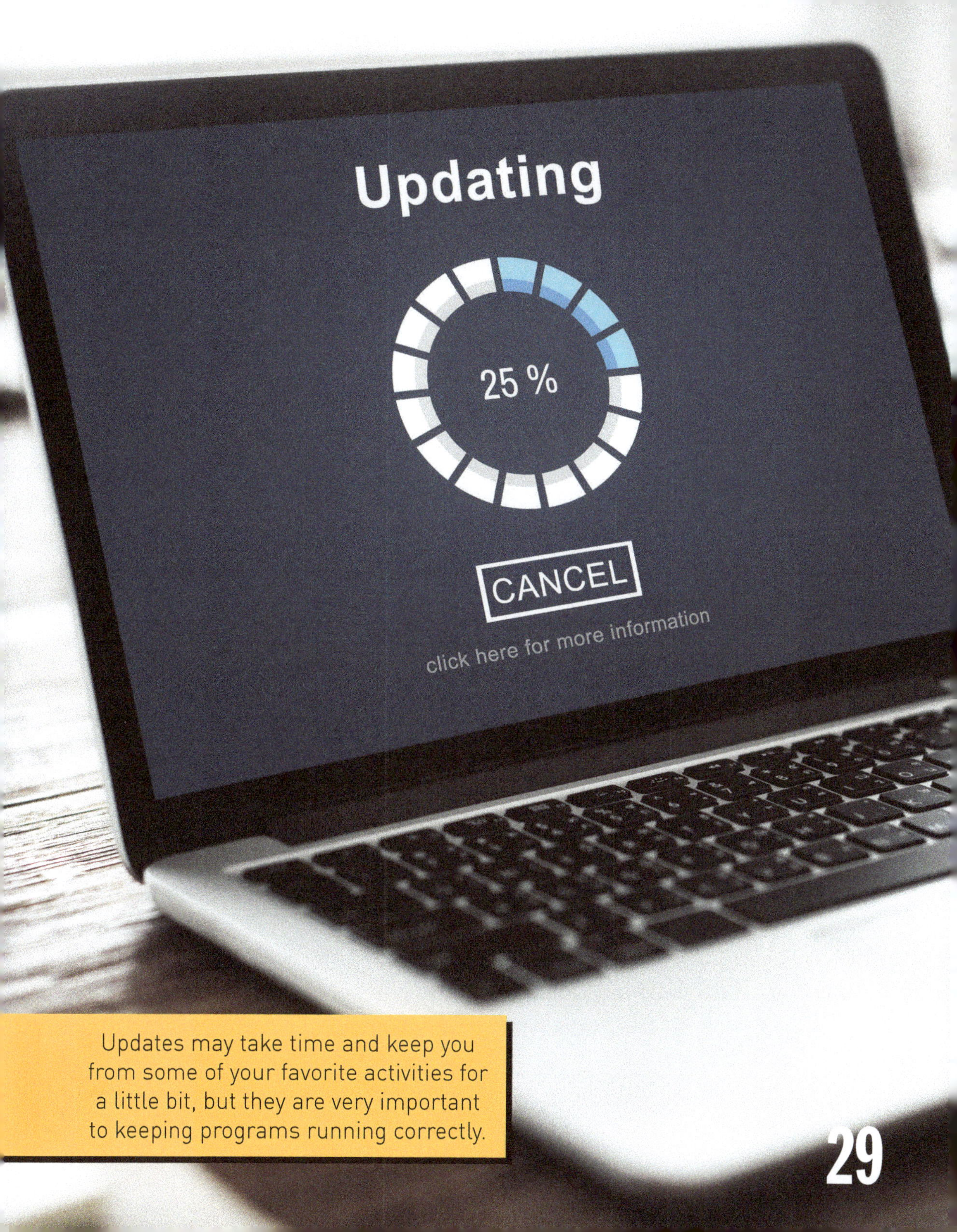

Updates may take time and keep you from some of your favorite activities for a little bit, but they are very important to keeping programs running correctly.

COMPUTER SCIENCE IS FULL OF TEAMWORK

Whether it's a huge project involving hundreds of people or a smaller project with only a few team members, the key ideas of planning, organization, communication, and teamwork are the same. Each programmer has the task of writing small amounts of code that may not do anything on their own. But when the whole team collaborates, all of the code comes together as a complete product.

From the project managers who make sure deadlines and requirements are met, to the software engineers and programmers who write code and tests, every person involved brings a unique skill to the team. And let's not forget the client who came up with the original idea—without that need for code, programmers would have nothing to program!

GLOSSARY

bug: An error in computer code.

client: A person who hires another person or company to complete a job.

code: The lines of text or symbols used to create a computer program.

code coverage: The amount of code that is tested.

collaborate: To work with others to complete something.

delegating: To assign tasks to others.

feedback: Helpful information or criticism that can be used to improve the project.

guidelines: A set of instructions that shows how something should be done.

pair programming: Two programmers working side by side, writing code together.

patch: A code update or correction to a computer program.

project scope: The overall detailed plan for a project.

scrum: A short meeting to discuss progress on a project.

software engineer: An experienced programmer who plans a project.

task: Something that must be done.

version control: A tool that keeps track of changes to a program or document.

INDEX

WEBSITES

Due to the changing nature of Internet links, PowerKids Press has developed an online list of websites related to the subject of this book. This site is updated regularly. Please use this link to access the list: www.powerkidslinks.com/eccs/collab